Chair Yoga for Seniors Over 60
Step By Step Guide

Introduction

As we grow older, exercising and doing yoga can become an absolute nightmare due to the gradual slowing down of various body processes. Despite this harsh reality, it is still in our best interest to engage in various exercises to keep our bodies and minds healthy and youthful.

Does aging mean seniors over 60 have no exercising avenues or that they cannot engage in restorative and healing yoga just because some muscles and joints hurt? No! It does not mean that because there's always chair yoga!

Not many people are aware of this great activity that accommodates the natural aging process and helps those with issues concerning mobility to work out and improve their mobility while at it.

Imagine enjoying all the benefits that come with exercising while staying comfortable and with minimum risk of hurting yourself. The benefits of chair yoga, especially for seniors, are too many to overlook.

If you're serious about reversing the aging process and taking advantage of all the benefits that come with exercising, but you're not sure where to start or how to go about chair yoga, this book is for you, so keep reading.

Chair Yoga for Seniors Over 60 will teach you a combination of perfectly crafted yoga poses and exercises that are great for people at all levels and that you can do in your chair at the comfort of your home, using only a few minutes a day.

Categorized into sections for each body part, the exercises or yoga poses in this book will help guarantee great posture and maximum physical and mental benefits!

First, let's start with what chair yoga is, how it works, and what makes it unique or different from regular yoga.

Section 1
Chair Yoga 101

Chair yoga is a derivation of the traditional yoga practice that comprises poses that go back over 5000 years ago. Most —if not all— of the poses found in classic yoga poses are replicable for chair yoga.

The chair yoga concept was coined because we spend a lot of time sitting at our desks or traveling from one place to another, so why not maximize the experience by engaging in a movement that can help increase circulation and exercise in our daily routine.

The same way the body moves through the flow of motion and increases flexibility when engaging in traditional yoga, chair yoga also helps actualize this. In addition to improving your range of motion, the widespread practice called pranayama (also known as breathing techniques) within chair yoga helps create spatial awareness. It also helps you practice meditation and reduces anxiety.

As the name suggests, you perform chair yoga from a sited, comfortable position. That is why the practice is ideal for the disabled or the elderly who are too old to stand up or exercise without hurting themselves. It is also great if you are suffering from conditions like osteoporosis, chronic pain, and multiple sclerosis.

The essence of the chair is to make sure you stay stable and don't strain your core as much when doing the exercises. Therefore, if you find the traditional yoga practice too stressful or tedious, you should try chair yoga to help you reap all the benefits of the practice.

But before we can start looking at the various chair yoga practices available for you to try, let's first look at the many benefits of chair yoga.

The Benefits Of Chair Yoga For Seniors

Traditional yoga poses have proven effective at dealing with various mental and physical problems. Since chair yoga is a variation of the standard yoga practice, the benefits are more likely the same, if not better, especially if you're a senior who can do nearly all the poses from the comfort of their seat.

Some of the great benefits you stand to gain from chair yoga include:

Helps in building strength

Any activity that involves using your muscles helps strengthen them as well. Therefore, each time you engage in yoga poses at the comfort of your seat, various muscle groups perform the activity, which helps build strength. Therefore, this means that the more you engage in different yoga practices, the more muscle strength you build.

When you build your strength, you also improve your balance which is very important in preventing falls. Additionally, the more muscle mass you build, the more calories you burn and the more bone density you gain, making daily activities a lot easier.

Helps in pain management

Most of the pain we experience, especially as seniors when doing various activities, results from the muscles not being strong or flexible enough to handle the pressure. Since these yoga practices help improve the flexibility and strength of your muscles, you will most likely not experience any pain when doing the activities.

This practice is also essential for people suffering from pain-related conditions like arthritis. It offers you various techniques such as deep breathing, gentle movement, and controlled visualization that help you cope with the pain and discomfort. This form of workout also encourages the body to produce feel-good hormones called endorphins that act as natural painkillers.

Helps reduce stress

Engaging in yoga requires focusing on your breathing, movement, and how your body works to perform the activity. This creates a moving meditation that helps reduce stress, promotes relaxation, and improves mental clarity. Like meditation, yoga helps promote a good mood, relieves anxiety and depression, and is great for boosting your confidence.
As mentioned above, any workout that helps the body produce feel-good hormones that act as natural stress relievers is great for relieving stress.

It helps improve flexibility

Chair yoga requires you to move and bend in many ways. Flexibility is of utmost importance because the exercises or poses adopted involve bending, twisting, and free movement. And even though the loss of flexibility usually happens due to old age, the fact is that you need to practice if you need to maintain your flexibility.
That is why chair yoga is important: it challenges your body to increase your range of motion and improve your mobility. The exercises involved are very useful for improving the flexibility of people at all levels and ages. The more you engage in these chair yoga exercises/poses, the more flexible you become.

Helps in weight management

Like any other form of exercise, chair yoga is quite effective for weight management. There are some poses or stretches that you may do while seated that can help your body burn more calories and build more muscles.
When you stretch your body to its limits, it starts using the fats stored in your body to help generate more energy required to keep your body healthy and strong. Therefore, the more yoga exercises you do, the more calories you burn and the more muscles you build.
Also, yoga is very useful for mindfulness and stress reduction, which are very important for improving nutritional choices and embracing a healthier lifestyle. If you'd like to lose weight in a more natural approach, you can try some specialized yoga poses that will help turn your body into a fat-burning machine.

It helps to improve awareness and mindfulness

When it comes to yoga poses or stretches, key things need to be in play if you're to benefit from the entire exercise.

Yoga is all about being aware of yourself and your surroundings and being in tune with them. Practicing chair yoga is a great way to improve that because it motivates you to bring awareness to your body and control your body and mind.

Having a heightened sense of awareness is great for promoting unity between your body and mind, mindful interaction with the world, and an increased sense of sense, all of which are great for the betterment of your life.

More precisely, chair yoga promotes deep breathing techniques that are key in helping you tune into what's going on in your body and stay grounded in the present.

It helps improve sleep

Most seniors experience insomnia. For you to get a good night's rest, you need to be calm so that your mind can slowly and peacefully transition into a trance state, where you're half-conscious so that you can sleep. However, this cannot happen when you're stressed or when your body is not in a rested condition.

By practicing chair yoga, you can utilize breathing and mindfulness techniques that help you relax and enter into a trance state easily and fast. Besides that, the stretches are great in ensuring that your body is in good condition to rest without any body aches or mobility issues. Chair yoga helps create a great environment that allows you to fall asleep more quickly and improves your quality of sleep.

It is a fun and engaging activity

In addition, to the many health benefits that chair yoga offers, one of the biggest benefits of chair yoga is that you get to engage in a fun and exciting activity with your peers, friends, loved ones, or even family members. Most seniors are usually bored from sitting idle all day; therefore, engaging in a fun activity is great for them. It helps you pass the time while you interact with your peers. It might even turn out to be your most exciting hobby yet!

These are some of the most important benefits you stand to gain from chair yoga. As you can see, these benefits are great for people of all ages and not just the elderly.

Next, let's look at some breathing and warm-up exercises you can engage in to make the whole process a lot easier.

Section 2
Warm-Ups

Warming up is very important when it comes to any physical activity. It is very important because it helps prevent injuries and enhances your body's performance. When you warm-up, blood flow to your muscles increases by up to 75%.

There is a tradition in yoga where you need to start with certain warm-ups, often known as vinyasa flows. The term vinyasa is often used to mean link breathing to movement. Most of the warm-up exercises are usually very short and will only take up about 10 minutes of your time.

Here are some of the quick and easy warm-up exercises for you to try:

#: Cat-Cow Pose

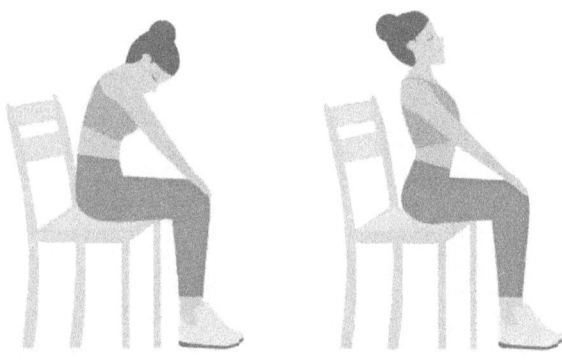

This easy pose is great for stretching and moving the joints of your spine and hips. The warm-up exercise requires you to sit in a comfortable chair and position.

Here is how to go about it.
1. Begin by sitting at an angle of 90 degrees with your back straight and facing forward.
2. Place your arms on your knees and take a deep breath.
3. Now slowly arch your back inwards until you're directly facing upwards as much as you can.
4. Remain in that position for 5 to 10 seconds before going back to your original position.
5. Repeat the same procedure about ten times until you feel your spine and hips are well stretched.

#: The Lotus Pose

Full Lotus Half Lotus Burmese

On a stool Seiza On a Chair

One of the greatest and easiest poses you can get into is the seated lotus pose. The purpose of this exercise is to help settle your mind as you open up your body to the other exercises and possess you're about to engage in.

Actually, most people recommend beginning with this technique before engaging in any exercise— if you meditate often, you might be more aware of this pose.

This is how you do it.

1. Start by making sure you're seated in a nice and comfortable position. You can add some cushions or a blanket to your seat.
2. If possible, try to cross your legs in front of each other. Make sure to cross them as much as you can. You can use your hands to push them as much as you can. However, be careful not to strain yourself.
3. Place your arms on your knees and gently rock back and forth while allowing your pelvis to tilt gently. As you move, try and find a place where your torso feels more natural.
4. Slowly breathe in and out until you feel your body is relaxed and your muscles opened up to more exercises.

#: Arms Upward Pose

The arms overhead pose is another great and easy warm-up exercise for you to try. The main idea behind this warm-up routine is to help stretch and strengthen your upper body parts, including your back, arms, and shoulders. You can easily do this pose in a seated or standing position.

Here is how you go about it.
1. The first step is to make sure you're seated in a comfortable position with your back straight and facing forward.
2. Take a deep breath and slowly bring both your arms forward until they are perpendicular to your chest.
3. Now slowly sweep your arms up while still stretched all the way out until they are straight and above your head.
4. Remain in that position for about 10 to 20 seconds before returning your arms to their original position.
5. Repeat the same procedure about 20 times without bringing your arms to their resting position.

#: Boat Pose

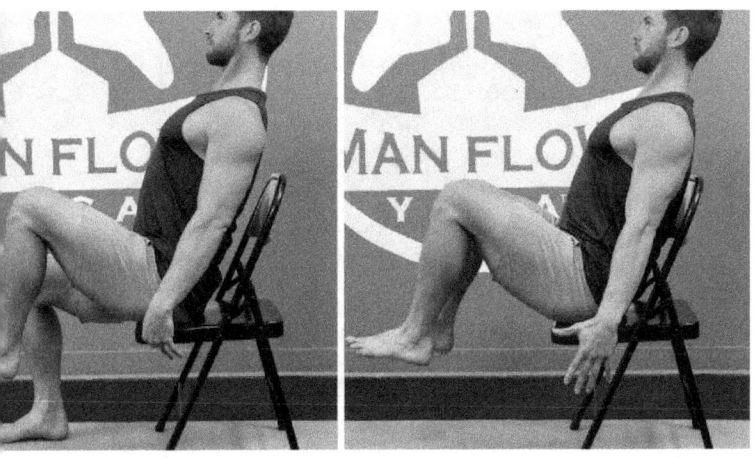

This is a more advanced but helpful form of warm-up exercise that is great for stretching your core muscles (stomach and back muscles) and your front leg muscles. The pose is good for beginners who have never done yoga before and those who are out of shape. If you have back problems, this is a great way to warm up.

Here is how to do it.
1. Start by sitting on the floor with your knees slightly bent and feet straight on the floor. Place your hands on the floor just alongside your hips.
2. Now gently bring your hands about a foot —or so— behind you while you bend your elbows a bit backward to provide enough support to hold your weight.
3. Slowly bring your ankles together while keeping your legs straight. Raise them from the floor slowly until you lean on your torso about 30 to 45 degrees.
4. Remain in that position for about 20 seconds before returning to your original position.
5. Repeat the same procedure about 20 times while maintaining a steady breath.

#: Sitting Twists

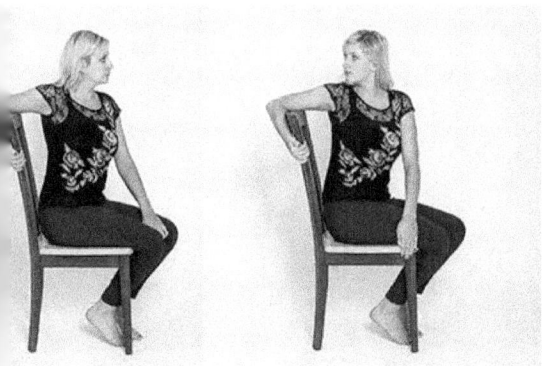

The sitting twists movement is a great warm-up routine that can help you gain some rotational movements into your spine to help improve your flexibility, strength, and motion. You can easily do the routine either when standing or sitting down.
Here is how to go about doing the exercise.
1. Start by sitting down in a comfortable position with your legs carefully crossed in front of you.
2. Now slowly twist your upper body towards the right until you are fully facing to your right but with your behind fully rooted down. Remain in that position for about 10 seconds.
3. Slowly move to your original position before twisting to your left side and posing in that position for about 10 seconds.
4. Ensure that you twist your upper body part as much as possible but without straining yourself too much.

#: Upward Plank Pose

Like the traditional plank pose, the upward plank pose is a variation of the traditional exercise routine that is great for warming up your core and leg muscles.
It is also great for opening up your chest, which helps ease your capacity to engage in and perform other exercises such as standing poses and more. This is a more advanced form of warm-up exercise, but anyone, even beginners, can manage to do it.
Here is how to go about it.
1. Start by sitting down comfortably with your legs stretched straight before you.
2. Now place your hands beside your hips before slowly taking them about an inch behind your back with your elbows slightly bent.
3. Make sure your hands are strong enough to hold your weight before lifting your torso slowly from the ground all the way up as much as possible.
4. Remain in that position for about 20 seconds before returning to your original position. Repeat this process about 20 times until you feel your core and leg muscles have become loose enough.

#: Leaning Forward Pose

The leaning forward pose warms up your core and leg muscles and is great for improving flexibility and mobility in your hips and spinal joints to help relieve any stiffness. It might be a bit more strenuous than other warm-up exercises, but it is great for getting you warmed up before you start working out.
Here is how you go about doing the exercise.
1. Start by sitting in the lotus position of your choice. Consider placing a blanket or a pillow underneath for maximum comfort.
2. Now lift your shin in front of the other and come into the pose, as illustrated in the picture. Make sure not to strain too much.
3. Push your arms as far as possible until you feel a slight tension in your back muscles. Stay in that position for about 20 seconds before going to your original position.
4. Repeat the same procedure several times until your core muscles and back feel well stretched.

#: Seated Shoulder Rolls

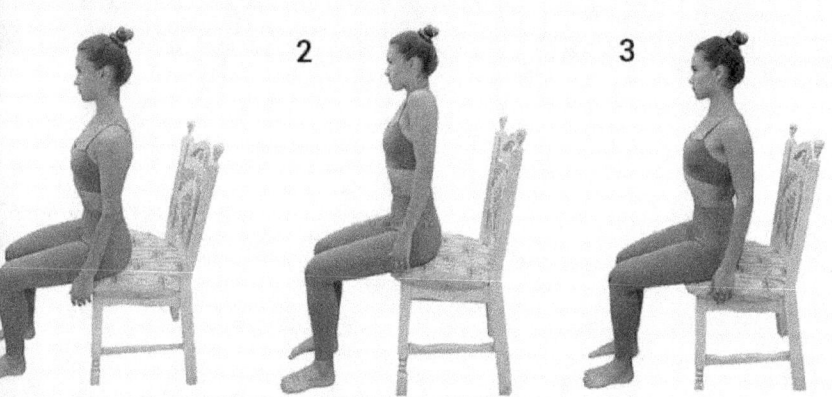

This is yet another easy warm-up routine that helps release the tension in your shoulder blades and upper arm muscle. The workout routine is easy enough for anyone to do, and it is great to help open up your muscles before starting your workout.
Here is how you go about doing the exercise.
1. Start by sitting down comfortably, with your back straight and legs at a ninety-degree angle.
2. Place your arms on your knees or thighs and take a deep breath.
3. Slowly shrug your shoulders forward and backward until you can draw a circle in the air with them.
4. Continue with the movements in a clockwise movement for about 30 seconds, then repeat the same in an anti-clockwise motion for another 30 seconds.

#: Seated Neck Stretches

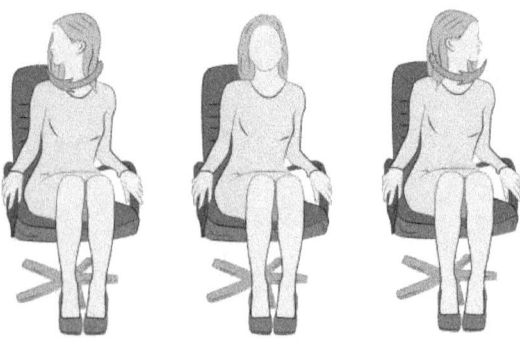

The neck muscles are one of the most forgotten muscles, yet they are greatly important to the whole workout routine. If you've experienced a stiff neck, then you're probably aware of how terrible it can feel not to have your neck muscles properly stretched out. This is a simple routine that almost everyone can do.
Here is how you do it.
1. Start by sitting comfortably on a chair with your back straight and facing forward.
2. Place your arms on your knees and take a deep breath.
3. Now slowly pull your head backward as you push your chest and spine outwards from your sitting bone to the top of your head.
4. Breathe out as you gently bring your head forward and your chin towards your sternum.
5. Now tilt your head from side to side until you can almost touch your shoulders with your ears.
6. Continue with the movements until you feel your neck is well stretched out.

#: Seated Side Stretches

This is yet another variation of the seated side twists but with the added advantage of stretching your arm muscles. This workout routine helps ensure that all the muscles in your upper body are well stretched out. It is quite easy, and you can do it in the comfort of your seat. This is how you do the pose.
1. Start by sitting down comfortably while facing forward and your back straight.
2. Take a deep breath, then lift your arms straight in the air.
3. While trying to make sure your behind is in contact with the seat, slowly shift your arms to your side such that the other side forms an outward curve. You can try and interlace your fingers if that feels more comfortable.
4. Now go back to your original position and exhale. Repeat the same procedure with your other side until you feel both sides are well stretched out.

Aside from these physical warm-up exercises, you can engage in breathing exercises that will help open up your airway and chest for the chair yoga workout you're going to do.

Section 3
Breathing Exercises

When you feel tired or worn out from a workout routine, most of the time, it's because your chest and body, in general, were not ready for the pressure. That is why you find yourself panting uncontrollably, even before you're halfway through the workout. That's why it's important to prepare your body for the massive or continuous breathing that will happen as you work out.

Here are some breathing exercises to help you get into the right mind frame and open up your body to the exercises you're about to engage in.

#: Square Breathing Movement

This breathing practice involves breathing in, breathing out, and holding your breath. These movements are supposed to be done in the same amount of time.

The idea of a square is to help make sure that you remember the breaths should be equal. This exercise is also therapeutic and can help you calm down and relax. Here is how you do it.

1. Sit comfortably with your back straight.
2. Place your arms on your knees or thighs, where you feel most comfortable.
3. Silently breathe in up to the count of four before holding your breath for another count of four.
4. Again, silently breathe out for a count of for before holding your breath for a similar amount of time.
5. Repeat this procedure for about 30 seconds or so.

#: Intentional Breathing

Being in control of your breathing is important because it helps you avoid getting worn out easily or fast while working out.

This breathing technique introduced by Dutch extreme athlete Wim Hof is great for boosting performance and optimizing health in general. The key thing with this exercise is the intention, not your body movements.

Here is how you go about it.

1. Make sure to sit in a nice and comfortable position.
2. Gently place your hands on your knees or thighs —wherever you feel most comfortable.
3. Slowly take a deep breath, then breath out; continue with this practice until you form a circular motion.
4. Continue the breathing patterns for about 30 to 40 cycles.
5. Once done with the last round, hold your breath in for as long as you can.

#: Twist Breaths

This breathing routine is great for increasing blood and air circulation to your core muscles. It is great for making sure your hands and feet are warm, especially if they normally get cold. If you know you're about to work out in the morning or are going to a cold place to work out, this technique would be very useful.

Here is how you do it.

1. Sit with your legs stretched out and as wide as possible.
2. Take slow and shallow breathes to help you calm down and relax.
3. Slowly begin to twist to your right as you allow your arms to move freely.

4. Make sure to breathe in as you center and exhale as you twist.
5. You can choose to lift your legs from the ground as you twist to make sure you're comfortable.
6. Continue alternating from left to right until you feel well stretched out.

#: The Skull Shining Breath

This is normally the go-to-practice when you want to warm up quickly and easily. It is a great warm-up routine that can help you feel energized and warm. This makes it the perfect warm-up exercise when you're feeling cold or sluggish or even when you want to work out in the morning.
Here is how you go about it.
1. Find a nice and comfortable place to sit and relax.
2. Place your arms on your thighs or knees —wherever you feel most comfortable.
3. Take a few deep and shallow breaths. Make sure to breathe fully through your nose and fully through your mouth.
4. Now take a deep breath and when you're three-quarters of the way through your nose, exhale sharply through your mouth. As you exhale, try to force the air out using your diaphragm and abdominal muscles.
5. Repeat this process for about 10 to 20 cycles while observing how you breathe.

#: Ujjayi Breath

Ujjayi, which means victorious, denotes the fact that each inhalation and exhalation is a celebration of life. The idea of this routine is to help ensure that you feel warm inside; it also keeps your mind focused on the present moment. It is quite unique in that you ought to feel and hear the whole process as you move. It is also referred to as the "oceanic breath" because if you listen closely to the cycles, you'll hear the sound of waves coming in and out of the shore.
Here is how you do it.
1. Find a comfortable position in which to sit while facing forward.
2. Place your hands on your sides somewhere on your knees or thighs.
3. Take a few breaths, then carefully rest your tongue behind the front of your teeth.
4. Inhale through your nose as you create a constriction at the back of your throat until you create a soft wheezing sound.
5. Try and keep the constriction at the back of your throat to help maintain the wheezing sound as you exhale.
6. Once done exhaling, push your navel into your stomach to remove any remaining air.

#: Bellows Breathing

Unlike the other forms of breathing, this is an intense breathing technique that involves a series of powerful inhalations and exhalations. This means if you have breathing problems or cannot handle vigorous breathing, you should not engage in this exercise. Otherwise, if you want to strengthen your circulation, you can try it.
Here is how to go about it.

1. Find a place to sit with your back resting on the backrest.
2. Place your arms on your torso and take a deep breath.
3. Now take a sharp and deep breath such that your diaphragm falls below until your lungs can't hold any more air.
4. Quickly and sharply let all the air out as quickly as possible, using your diaphragm to remove any remnant air.
5. Hold your breath for about 10 seconds before repeating the steps above for about four rounds of ten breaths.

#: Cooling Breaths

Another great breathing technique that can prove very useful for calming down and focusing your thought is the cooling breaths. Also known as Seetakari, this breathing routine is great for people who always feel hot or warm, even on a chilly day.
If you'd like to easily and quickly cool down, then you can try this breathing routine. It is also great for cooling you down when you're sick or experiencing a fever or hot flushes and would like to cool down.
Here is how you go about it.
1. Find a comfortable place to sit and place your arms on your knees.
2. Close your eyes and gently take a deep breath.
3. Gently bring your upper and lower teeth together while allowing your lips to come apart.
4. Slowly and deeply through the space in your teeth until you make a hissing sound.
5. Now close your lips and expel the air through your nose for about 10 minutes and slowly increase the pace in intervals of 5 minutes.

#: Alternate Nostril Breathing

This is one of the easiest yogic deep breathing because it is simple and straight to the point. It doesn't require much work because your fingers will do the work for you. It is great for inducing slow rhythmic breathing that is great for calming down, and when you switch the sides, it involves both sides of your brain.
Here is how you do it.
1. Find a comfortable position to sit in with your back straight.
2. Using your right thumb, close your right nostril and then place your index and middle finger between your eyebrows as your small finger dangles in the air.
3. Exhale completely using your left nostril and gradually allow the air back in. Once the inhalation reaches its peak, quickly release the left nostril and close your right nostril. You can now exhale through the right nostril and continue alternating for about ten rounds.

#: Lion's Breath

This is a great yogic breathing technique that is very useful for relieving tension in your face and chest. It is also known as Simsahana or lion's pose, and it is easy to do. The breathing technique is also relaxing and soothing.
Here is how you do it.

1. Find a comfortable place to sit and relax.
2. Place your arms on your knees or thighs, with your fingers spread out.
3. Open your eyes wide and take a deep breath.
4. As you do step 3, open your mouth and stick your tongue out as much as you can while making sure to bring it as close as possible to your chin.
5. Now tighten your throat muscles and exhale through your mouth as you make the 'ha' sound.
6. You can even try to look at the tip of your nose or the middle of your eyebrows as you do it.
7. Repeat the procedure for about 2 to 3 breaths.

#: Focus Breathing Technique

This is yet another breathing technique that helps you become more centered and aware of your breathing. It usually involves the use of phrases and focus words. The process is more like hypnotherapy, but the purpose is to make you feel more calm and relaxed.

To perform this technique, you need to find a word that makes you calm or happy. It can be any word as long as your mind can focus on it and bring you some sense of belonging or focus.

Here is how you go about performing this routine.
1. Begin by sitting down in a nice and comfortable place.
2. Slowly focus your mind on your breathing without changing how you're breathing.
3. Gradually shift from your normal to deep breathing, then back to normal breathing. Take note of the movements in your abdomen as you breathe.
4. You can try placing your hand on your lower belly to notice how it rises and falls as you breathe.
5. As you breathe out, ensure you exhale all the air from your lungs.
6. As you alternate between normal and deep breathing, focus on the word or phrase you chose to help make sure you're relaxed as much as possible.
7. Imagine that the air you're breathing removes all the negativity and health problems you might be having.

This chapter has discussed some of the main chair yoga breathing exercises you can engage in to gain the most from the process. It is also advisable to incorporate these breathing techniques with chair yoga warm-up exercises to help prepare your body for the intensive workout.

Now let's look at some of the best chair yoga exercises you can try, all grouped according to the specific muscle groups they affect.

Section 4
Chair Yoga Poses For Seniors

The good thing with chair yoga is that there is a pose or exercise especially suited for all body muscles. It is important to reach every muscle in your body because it ensures that you work on all muscles. There are also chair yoga poses that suit people of all levels, whether you're a pro or a beginner.

Here are some of the best chair yoga poses for seniors:

#: Seated Mountain Pose

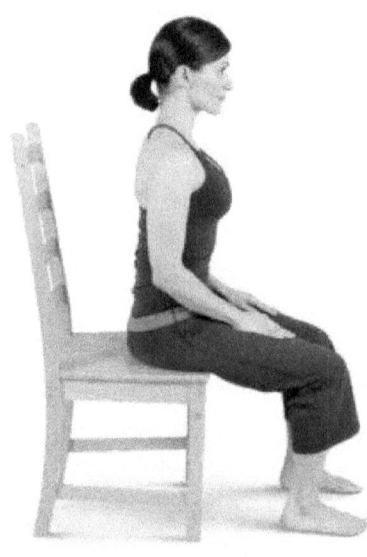

The first pose you can do is the seated mountain pose. It is usually a very simple pose that is perfect for engaging your core and focusing your breath. It is usually the first pose you will most likely do every time you need to perform any chair yoga routine.

Here is how you do it.
1. While sitting down, take a deep breath and lengthen your spine as much as possible.
2. Slowly breathe out as you push your sitz bone (the bottom of your pelvis) into the chair. Make sure you form a 90-degree angle with your thighs, back, and legs.
3. Again, take a deep breath, then slowly exhale as you push your shoulders down and back. Make sure to engage your core muscles and relax your arms by your side.
4. Remain in that position for about 10 seconds as you breathe normally.

#: Chair Forward Bend

This yoga pose might be a tad strenuous for people with back problems, but it is great for stretching your core and back muscles. It enables you to be as flexible as possible while being as comfortable as possible, making it a lot easier. Therefore, if you've been having back problems, then this chair yoga pose can help lengthen your spine and reduce the tension in your back muscles.

Here is how you go about it:
1. Start by sitting down comfortably with your back straight.
2. Place your arms on your knees or thighs and take a deep breath.
3. Bring your palms together before your pelvic area and spread your legs apart.
4. Now slowly bend down with your hands before you until they touch the floor between your feet.
5. Remain in that position for about 10 seconds before going back to your original position.
6. Repeat the same procedure for about 20 to 30 reps.

#: One-Sided Arm Lifts

This chair yoga pose is great for strengthening your lungs, chest, and shoulders while engaging your abs, making it a great workout routine for strengthening your upper body muscle.

The exercise routine is very involving and a bit advanced, but it is great for opening up your body muscles. It is a variation of the forward lean pose but more effective.

Here is how you do it:
1. Start by sitting down in a nice and comfortable place.
2. Gradually bend into the forward bend position, then take a deep breath.
3. With your hands on the floor, slowly engage your chest and twist to your left as you exhale.
4. Slowly lift your left arm as much as possible, then look up at your arm.
5. Remain in that position for about 20 seconds as you maintain your breathing.
6. Go back to your original position and repeat the same procedure with your right side.

#: Seated Pigeon Pose

The seated pigeon pose is a great workout routine that helps strengthen your groin, glutes and leg muscles while stimulating your digestive system. As the name suggests, the pose imitates a position that most pigeons tend to assume. This beginner-friendly pose doesn't require much work.

Here is how you do the pose.
1. Start by comfortably sitting down with your arms on your knees or thighs.
2. Take a deep breath before holding your left ankles with both hands.
3. Slowly lift your left leg sideways towards your right knee as you breathe out.
4. Place your left ankle to rest on your right thigh or knee, then remain in that position for about 20 seconds.
5. Return your leg to its original position before repeating the same procedure with your right leg.

#: Reverse Arm Hold

The reverse arm hold is a great and easy workout routine that helps open up your chest and stretch your arm muscles. It is also great for helping you relax and calm down. The best part about the pose is that it is beginner-friendly and can be done by nearly everyone at any place as long as you're seated.

Here is how you do the pose:
1. Start by finding a comfortable place to sit while ensuring your back is straight.
2. Take a deep breath, then stretch both your arms by your side as much as possible.
3. Bring both your arms back, then bend them at your elbow such that your right arm can touch your left elbow and vice versa.
4. Slowly clasp your hands together and gently add some resistance by pulling your arms upwards.
5. Remain in that position for about 20 seconds before returning to your original position.

#: Arm Spiral Pose

The arm spiral pose is a beginner-friendly chair yoga workout routine that is great for opening up your shoulders, stretching your arms, and improving the circulation in your body. At a glance, you might think that the pose is just a waste of time and energy, but it is quite effective if you do it the right way.
Here is how you go about doing the pose:
1. Start by sitting down in a nice, comfortable place with your back straight.
2. Take a deep breath, then bring both your arms forwards.
3. Carefully wrap both your arms around each other as much as you can until you form a spiral.
4. Slowly try to grab your shoulders with opposite hands as if you're hugging yourself.
5. Lift your elbows and remain in that position for about 20 seconds.
6. Go back to your original position before doing the pose anti-clockwise.

#: Seated Star Pose

The seated star pose is one great workout routine that involves most of the muscles in your body. It is great for lengthening, strengthening, and aligning your spine and body. It is also beginner-friendly and can be done by just about anyone.

Here is how you go about it:
1. Start by sitting down in a nice comfortable place with your back straight
2. Place your hands on your knees or thighs, then take a deep breath.
3. Slowly extend your arms to your side as much as possible, then lift them.
4. Now gradually spread your legs wide and lift them as much as you can as well.
5. Hold your breath for 2 minutes and remain in that position for 2 minutes as well.
6. Go back to your original position, then repeat the procedure for ten to twenty reps.

#: Seated Warrior

If you're looking for a more advanced form of chair yoga, then the seated warrior is perfect for you. Even though it is quite involving, it is very beneficial because it helps strengthen your core muscles, glutes, and leg muscles. It is also very helpful in improving circulation in your body.

Here is how you do it.

1. Start by sitting down in a nice and comfortable place. Consider placing a pillow or a blanket for this pose.
2. Take a deep breath and slowly twist to your right such that your right leg is on the right side of the seat and your left leg is stretched straight behind you.
3. Bring your hands straight forward, then exhale slowly as you lift them straight into the air.
4. Remain in that position for about 20 seconds before returning to your original position.
5. Repeat the same procedure with the opposite side.

#: One Leg Stretch

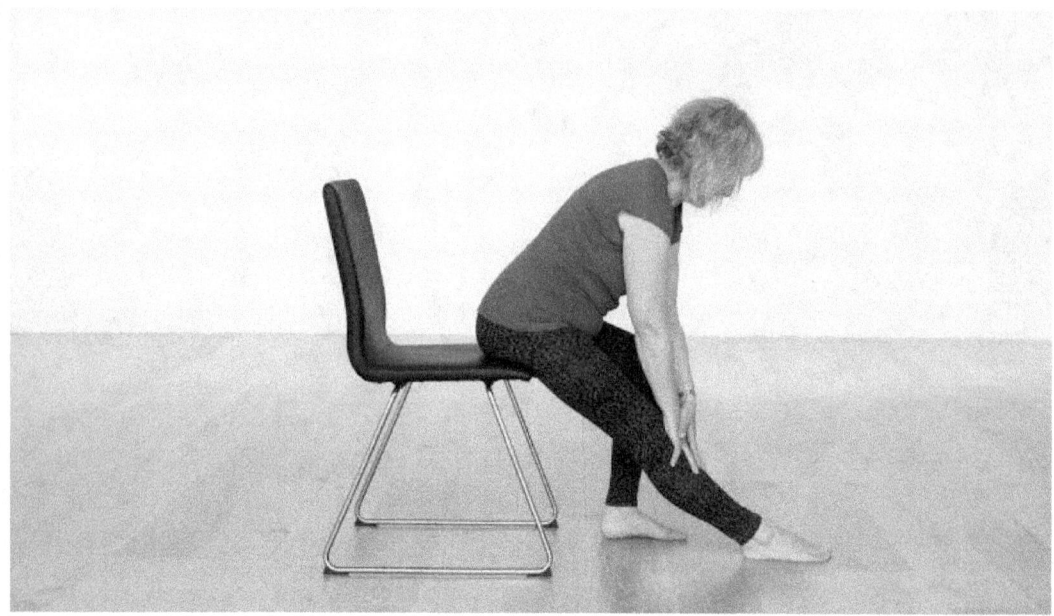

The One Leg Stretch pose is excellent for stretching and lengthening your spine and leg muscles. It is almost similar to the forward bend lean pose but slightly different. It might be a bit strenuous for you or people with back problems, but it is great for improving your body's circulation. The pose is quite easy to do if you put in enough effort or push yourself —don't overdo it.
Here is how you go about doing this chair yoga pose:
1. Begin by sitting down comfortably with your back straight and your hands on your knees or thighs.
2. Take a deep breath, then slowly bring your left leg forward.
3. While keeping the right leg bent, lean down slowly until you can touch your left leg toes with your left hand.
4. Stretch as much as possible, then remain in that position for about 20 seconds before returning to your original position.
5. Repeat the same procedure with your other side, then remember to exhale fully as you go back to your original position.
6. Do this procedure for about 20 to 30 reps.

#: Shoulder Circle Rolls

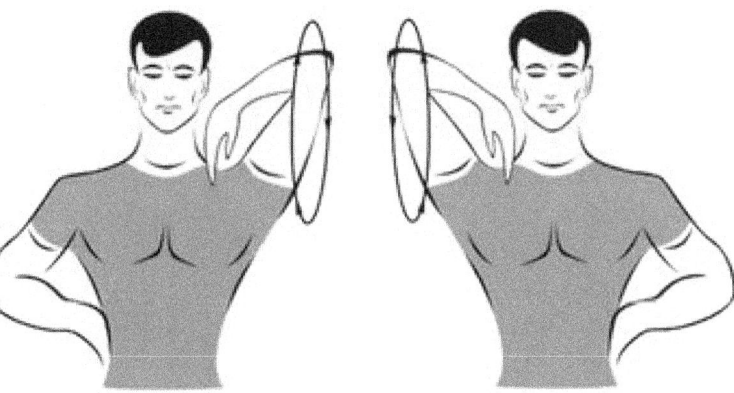

This exercise strengthens your upper back muscles and improves flexibility in the shoulder blades. It is quite easy and beginner-friendly but great for improving circulation and relieving your arm muscles of any tension build-up. It is advisable to do this exercise earlier on in your workout routine.
Here is how you do it.
1. Sit comfortably in a nice and comfortable seat with your back straight and facing forward.
2. Take a deep breath, then place the tips of your fingers on top of your shoulders.
3. Slowly lift your shoulders up and forward, then immediately bring them down and backward until you form circles with your shoulders.
4. Do this for about 20 seconds in a clockwise manner before changing into an anti-clockwise manner.
5. Keep doing the same for about 20 reps until you feel your shoulders and arm muscles are well stretched.

#: Seated Side Stretch Pose

This is a variation of the seated side twists, but it is more involving. This chair yoga pose is great for stretching your back muscles and straightening your spine as well. It is quite easy, and you can do it comfortably as long as you're seated. It is also great for improving circulation in your body.

Here is how to go about it:
1. Start by finding a comfortable place to sit and ensure your back is straight and leaning against the backrest.
2. Take a deep breath, then slowly move your left arm towards your right side as much as you can while making sure your behind stays glued to your seat.
3. Slowly exhale as you turn towards your right side, and remain in that position for 20 seconds before moving to your original position.
4. Continue with the side-to-side movements until your back feels well stretched and your spine is well aligned.
5. Continue with the movements for about 20 seconds. Make sure to exhale as you move back to your original position.

#: Chair Neck Rolls

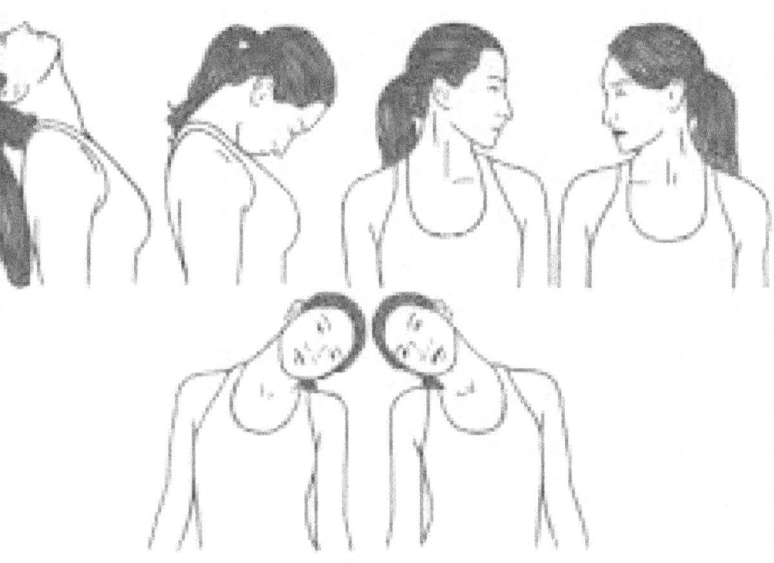

The neck muscles are usually overlooked in most workouts, but most people forget that neck muscles are very important.

They are supposed to be constantly stretched to help prevent stiff necks, which are usually very painful and uncomfortable. It also helps ensure that your spine is well aligned, with proper circulation happening in your head. This technique might seem simple, but it can work wonders on your nervous system when you incorporate breathing techniques.

Here is how to do yoga neck rolls.

1. Begin by sitting down comfortably with your back straight and facing forward.
2. Take a deep breath, then take your neck upwards and backward as much as you can, then exhale as you bring your neck down to your chin.
3. Continue with the back and forward movements for about 20 seconds while making sure to stretch your neck muscles as much as you can.
4. Once you go back to your original position, shift your neck towards your left such that your left ear is touching your left shoulder. Remain in that position for about 10 seconds before going back to your original position.
5. Repeat the same procedure with your right side but make sure to utilize breathing techniques as you do so.
6. Once done with steps four and five, slowly tilt your face to the right as much as possible before tilting your face again to the left as much as possible.
7. Continue with the movements for about 20 seconds before tilting your head in a circular motion as you wind up.

#: Supported Forward Bend Pose

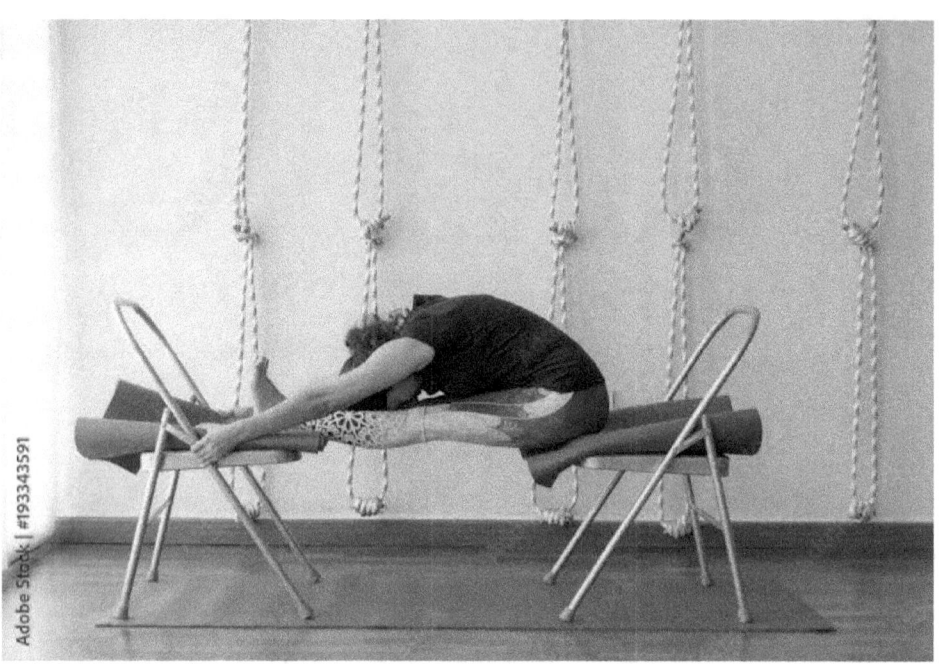

For this pose, you'll need to have two seats or a place to place your legs while doing it. It is a variation of the forward lean bend, but it is more demanding and effective at enhancing flexibility and releasing tension. This workout is also great for aligning your spine and strengthening your leg muscles.

Here is how you go about doing it.
1. Start by placing two seats facing each other and close together.
2. Sit down in one of the two chairs and place your legs on the other chair in front of you.
3. Make sure you're comfortable, then take a deep breath before leaning forward until you can touch your toes with your fingertips.
4. Go as low as possible; if you can touch your ankles, the better.
5. Remain in that position for about 30 seconds before returning to your original position.
6. Continue with the movements for about 20 reps until your back muscles are well stretched.

#: Seated Half-Forward On Toes Pose

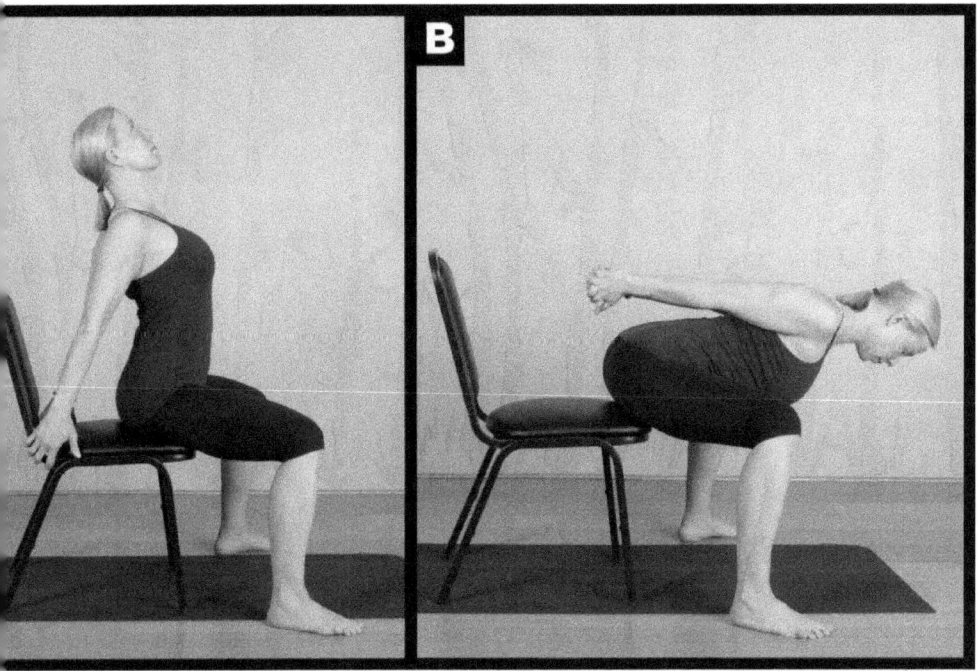

If you'd like to make your chair yoga workout routine more interesting, this is the pose for you. This is another variation of the forward lean bend pose, but it is a tad easier to do. The pose is great for strengthening arm muscles, hips, core muscles, and feet. It is also great for improving circulation in the body.

Here is how you go about doing the pose.
1. Start by sitting down in a nice and comfortable place.
2. Take a deep breath, then bring both your arms forward.
3. Slowly lift them up as you breathe out as much as possible, then lean forward a bit.
4. Raise your feet such that you're supporting yourself with your toes and remain in that position for about 20 seconds.
5. You can try and bend your elbows to form 90 degrees with your arms.

#: Hand Clenches

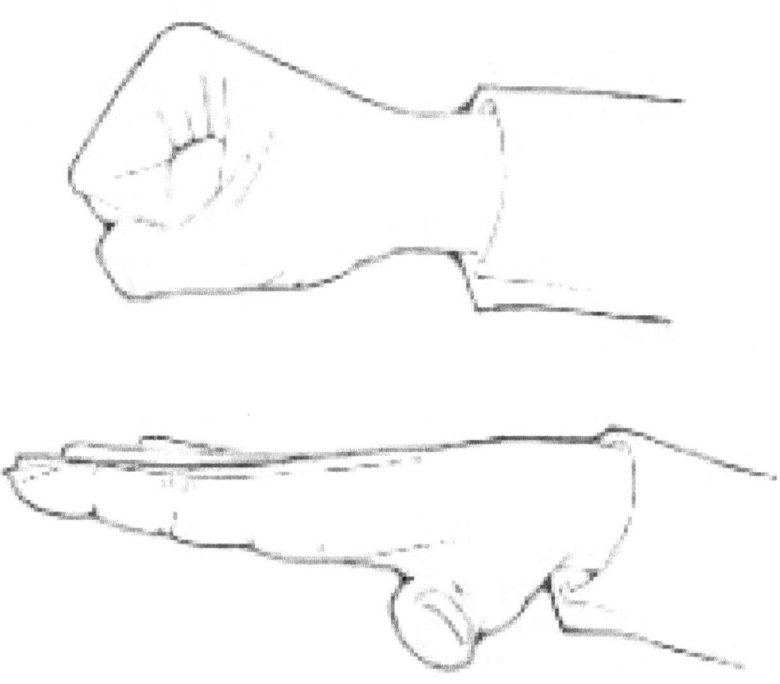

This easy chair yoga pose is great for preparing your body for an intense workout or increasing blood circulation to your arms. It is also great for strengthening your arms and shoulder muscles while improving flexibility. Hand clenches are beginner-friendly and can be done just about anywhere as long as you're seated comfortably.
Here is how you do it.
1. Start by sitting down in a nice, comfortable place with your back straight and facing forward.
2. Take a deep breath, then slowly lift your arms forward as straight as possible.
3. Exhale, then open up your palms by spreading out your fingers.
4. While still in that position, make a fist on both hands, then release; make a fist again, then release. Make sure to clench your fist as much as possible and keep your hands straight and perpendicular, don't lower them!
5. Continue making a fist and releasing it until you feel no tension in your arms.

#: Cactus Raised Arms Pose

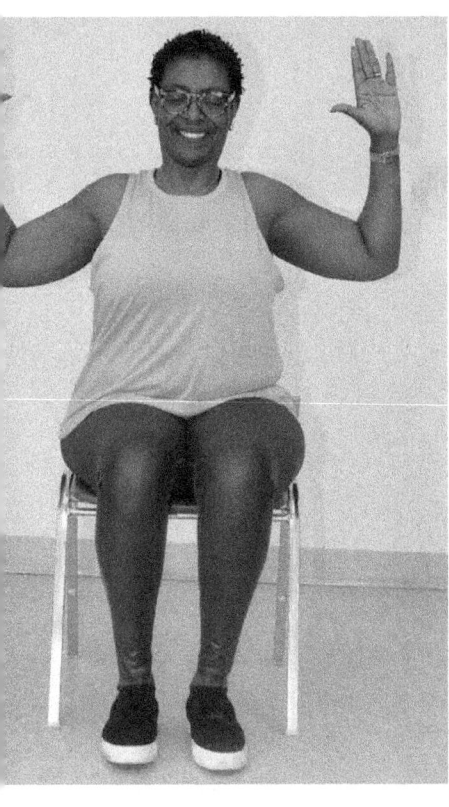

This is a good startup workout routine that improves your circulation and flexibility, preparing you for more intense workout routines. The cactus raised arms pose is great for strengthening your arms, shoulders, and chest muscles. It is also beginner-friendly and can be done by just about anyone.

Here is how to go about doing this chair yoga pose.
1. Start by sitting down in a nice, comfortable position while facing forward.
2. Inhale, and while keeping your spine straight, extend your arms wide and push your chest outwards.
3. Once you extend your arms straight beside you, bend your elbows and lift your hands to form 90 degrees with your arms.
4. Remain in that position for 20 to 30 seconds before returning to your original position.
5. Repeat the same procedure for about 20 reps.

#: Goddess Pose

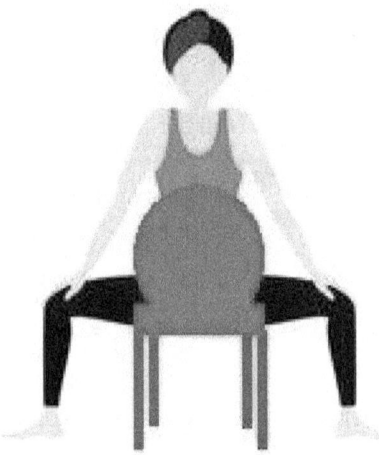

This is a great beginner-friendly workout routine that helps improve circulation and flexibility. It also helps strengthen the hips, knees, and pelvic muscles.
Here is how you do it.
1. Start by sitting down comfortably but instead of facing forward, sit while facing backward.
2. Spread your legs as wide as possible with your feet pointing out.
3. Hold the backrest for support, then inhale and exhale normally.
4. Hold that position for about 20 seconds before loosening your legs and stretching them forward.
5. If you're up for a challenge, you can push back into a squat behind the chair and hold on to it for support.
6. Remember to keep your breathing normal as you perform the workout routine.

#: Half-Moon Pose

Unlike the other chair yoga poses, this one requires you to stand on your feet; however, you'll still rely on the chair for support. This workout routine is great for strengthening many muscles in your body, such as the chest, hamstrings, upper back and shoulders, core and arm muscles. The pose is also great for improving circulation and flexibility.
Here is how you go about doing the workout.
1. Start by standing straight in front of the seat.
2. Inhale, then slowly lower your body until you touch the seat with your hands. Go lower again until you place your forearm on the seat.
3. Use your right hand for support, then raise your left hand.
4. Slowly lift your left leg until it is perpendicular to your body. Ensure you're balanced, with your right forearm is offering enough support.
5. Remain in that position for about 20 seconds before returning to your original position.
6. Repeat the same procedure with your left side.

#: Chair Sit-Ups

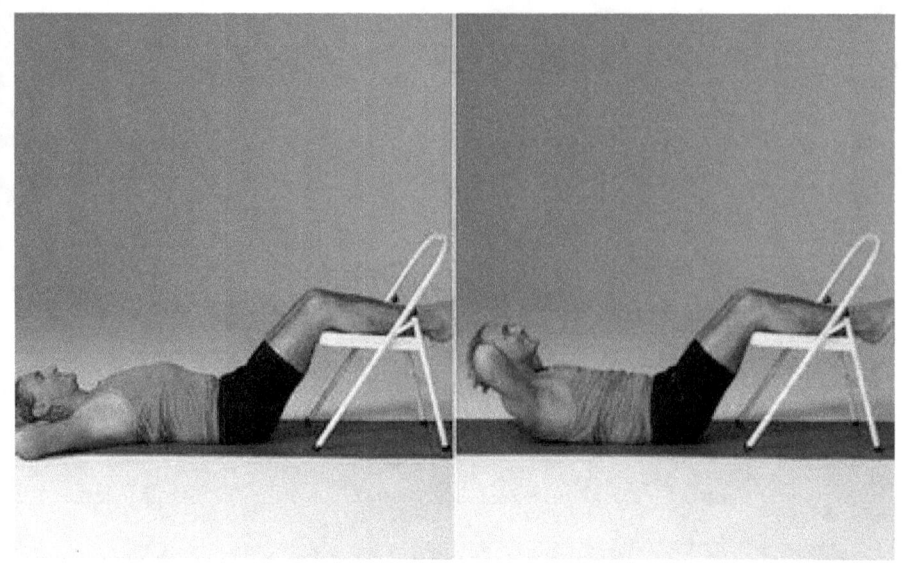

Sit-ups are a common workout routine for most people. They have proven to be very effective, and these chair sit-ups are no exception. They help boost your energy and strengthen your core muscles, especially your abs. Chair sit-ups are great for improving circulation and opening your body for an intense workout. The only difference between this and the normal sit-ups most people know is that for this, you'll need a chair.
Here is how you do it.
1. Place a chair in front of you, then lie down while facing forward.
2. Bring your legs up and place them on the seat. Move as close as possible to the seat such that your legs form 90 degrees.
3. With your arms beside you, take a deep breath and exhale, then slowly bring them behind your head.
4. Interlock your fingers before taking a deep breath. Slowly lift your head as much as possible with the aim of reaching your thighs or knees with your forehead.
5. Once you reach for your thighs or knees as much as possible, go back to laying down flat and exhale.
6. Repeat the same procedure for about twenty reps. You can try alternating from left to right as you do the sit-ups.

#: Reverse Warrior Pose

This is another variation of the normal warrior pose, but it is more involving and strenuous. This chair yoga pose is great for strengthening almost all the muscle groups in your body, such as the neck, upper back, hamstrings, chest, knees, and hips. It is also great for improving flexibility and circulation in your body.

Here is how you go about doing the exercise.
1. Start by sitting down in a nice and comfortable position; consider placing a pillow or a cushion on the seat.
2. Take a deep breath, then slowly shift your right leg to the right side of your seat to form 90 degrees, then stretch your left leg behind you.
3. Exhale, then shift your upper body to face your right side.
4. Once you enter into the warrior position, shift your back backward until you can touch your left leg with your left arm, then raise your right hand in the air.
5. See the image above for a more accurate illustration of what to do.

#: Crescent High Lunge Twists

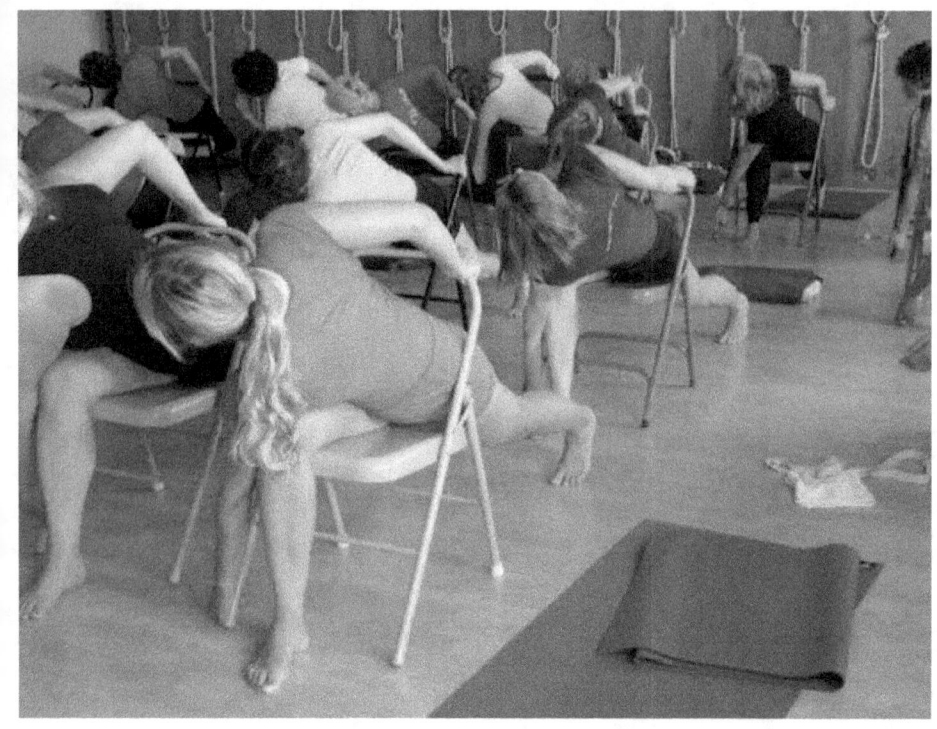

The crescent high lunge twists are great for strengthening the hips, gluteus, upper back, shoulders, and arms. This workout routine is also great for improving circulation and flexibility of your joints, and it helps stretch the muscles in your body. The workout routine is a bit more strenuous than most other chair yoga poses, but it is quite effective and beneficial. It is a variation of the side chair twists but more advanced.
Here is how to go about it.
1. Start by sitting down comfortably with your face forward.
2. Take a deep breath, then bring your right leg to the right side of your seat and stretch your left leg behind you to the left of the chair.
3. Exhale and gradually twist your upper body towards your right until you can hold the backrest with both your arms while your face is facing backward.
4. Remain in that position for about 20 seconds before returning to your original position.
5. Repeat the same procedure with your other side, then keep alternating for 20 reps.

#: Extended Side Marichi Pose

This pose doesn't require you to sit, but you still need a chair. The workout is great for strengthening muscles such as the chest, hamstrings, arms and shoulders, hips, and back. It is also great for improving flexibility, strength, and balance.

Here is how to go about doing it.
1. Start by standing right in front of the chair as close as possible.
2. Place your right leg on the seat and grab onto the backrest with your left hand.
3. Slowly lift your right arm as high as possible, then tilt your face to look upwards.
4. Remain in that position for about 20 seconds before returning to your original position.
5. Repeat the same procedure with your left side and keep alternating from side to side for 20 reps.

#: Bolster Head Arms Pose

This is a beginner-friendly workout routine that helps strengthen the arms and shoulders, hips external, back and knees. It is also a very comfortable chair yoga pose that helps improve flexibility, balance, and circulation in your body. This chair yoga pose is a variation of the praying Buddha pose, but you will need a chair that will act as the support system. Here is how you can go about doing it.

1. Start by sitting down close to a chair facing you.
2. Place a pillow or a blanket below you then cross your legs as shown in the picture below.

3. Place both your arms on the seat and fold them.
4. Slowly lean forward and rest your head at the back of your hands.
5. Stay in that position for about 20 seconds before goings back to your original position.
6. Make sure to inhale and exhale during the entire process.

#: Downward Facing Plank Pose

The Downward Facing Plank pose is a variation of the famous plank pose. It is an advanced form of workout routine that helps strengthen muscles in your body, such as the gluteus, hips, and psoas. It is a very beginner-friendly workout routine and is best suited for people who cannot do the normal plank.

Here is how you do the pose.
1. Start by standing up straight behind a chair, with the backrest facing you.
2. Make sure you're a few inches from the chair and hold the backrest with both arms.
3. Lower your upper body part as low as you can until you're facing the floor and forming 90 degrees with the chair.
4. With the support of the chair, raise your body as much as you can until you form a diagonal and stand on your toes.
5. Remain in that position for about 20 seconds before returning to your original position.

6. Repeat the same procedure for about 20 reps.

#: Chair Gate Pose

The chair gate pose is a variation of the sideways pose we discussed earlier, but the pose is more strenuous and effective. It is a beginner-friendly workout routine that helps strengthen the core, arm, and leg muscles while also helping improve flexibility and balance.
Here is how you do the pose.

1. Begin by sitting down comfortably with your face forward.
2. Place your arms on your thighs or your knees and take a deep breath.
3. Slowly extend your left leg out as much as you can.
4. Gradually twist your upper body sideways until you can touch your left leg with your left hand as you stretch your right arm upwards.
5. Remain in that position for about 20 seconds before returning to your original position.
6. Repeat the same procedure with your right side and keep alternating for ten reps.

#: Standing Forward Fold Pose

This is the perfect pose if you'd like to make your workout routine a little more challenging. It might be a bit strenuous, but it is quite effective in strengthening your muscles, improving flexibility, and improving balance. Some of the muscles it helps to strengthen are the abs, arms and shoulders, neck, hip externals, and back muscles.

Here is how you go about doing this chair yoga pose.

1. Start by standing in front of the chair you intend to use.
2. Slowly lift your left leg and place it on the seat, then turn and face your right side.
3. Take a deep breath, then lower your upper body as much as you can until you can use your right arm to touch your right foot.
4. Place your left arm on the seat to help improve your stability and posture.
5. Remain in that position for about 20 seconds before returning to your original position.
6. Repeat the same procedure with your other side.

#: Seated Wind Release Pose

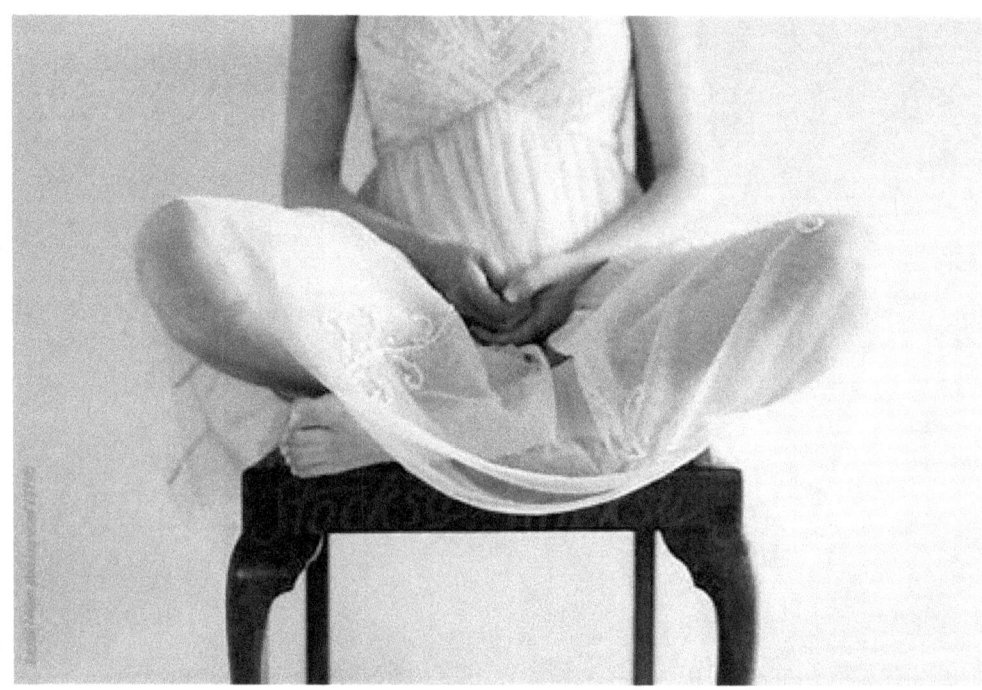

This is another beginner-friendly chair yoga workout that helps strengthen your muscles and opens up your body in preparation for the workout. Some of the muscles targeted by this pose include the legs, gluteus, back, and arm muscles. It is quite easy to do and can be done by just about anyone from the comfort of their seat. It is also great for improving flexibility and circulation in your lower body muscles.

Here is how you go about doing the exercise.

1. Start by sitting down in a nice, comfortable place, with your back straight and facing forward.
2. Take a deep breath, then carefully lift both your legs up as much as you can. Make sure to keep your back straight.
3. Wrap your arms around your legs for support, then remain in that position for about 20 seconds.
4. Exhale and go back to your original position. Repeat the same procedure for about 15 reps.
5. There are variations to this pose where you can alternate raising one leg after the other. You can repeat the same procedure but instead of raising both legs, raise one leg after the other while using both your arms for support.
6. *Remember to breathe normally and stay in that position for about 20 seconds before alternating with the other leg.*

#: Camel Pose With Chair

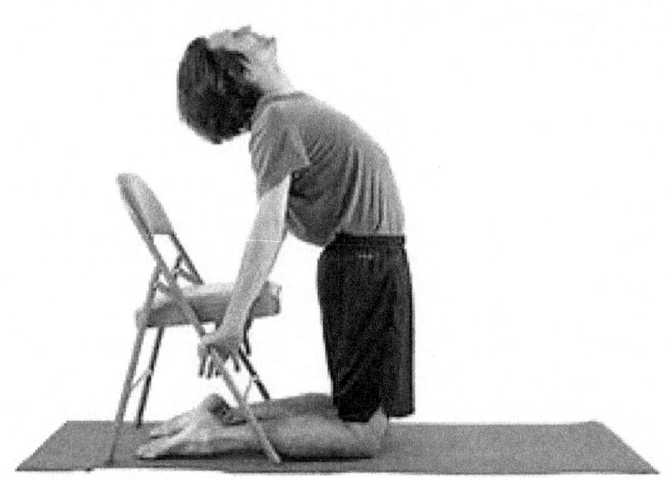

There are several variations of this pose, but the one in focus here is the camel chair pose. This is a very simple but effective yoga pose that is great for improving flexibility and circulation in your body.
The camel pose with chair pose is great for strengthening a wide range of muscles in the body, such as the back, hips, arms, and core muscles. It is the less strenuous form of the normal camel pose that requires you to go all the way down to your feet.
Here is how you go about doing the pose.
1. Begin by standing close to a chair but with your back facing it. Make sure to stand a few inches from the chair to give enough room to your legs once you kneel.
2. Carefully kneel and bring your arms backward such that they can hold the seat behind you.
3. Now slowly lean back as much as you can until you face upwards. Make sure to keep your feet together and in between the chair.
4. Remain in that position for about 20 seconds before returning to your original position. Repeat this process for ten reps while making sure you bend backward as much as possible.

#: Supported Chair Camel Pose

The supported chair camel pose is a variation of the camel pose we discussed earlier, but this pose is easier in comparison. It is a beginner-friendly workout routine that helps improve flexibility and strengthens the chest, arms and shoulders, neck and knee muscles. The pose is also great for improving circulation in your body and preparing you for a workout.
Here is how you go about doing the pose.
1. Start by standing next to a chair, with your back facing the chair and a few inches from the chair.
2. Carefully bring your arms backward and lower your right hand until it reaches the seat, then immediately lower your other arm to reach the seat.
3. Make sure to go as lower as possible then remain in that position for about 20 seconds before going back to your original position
4. Make sure to keep your breathing normal and continue with the process for about ten reps.

#: The Forward Bend Pose

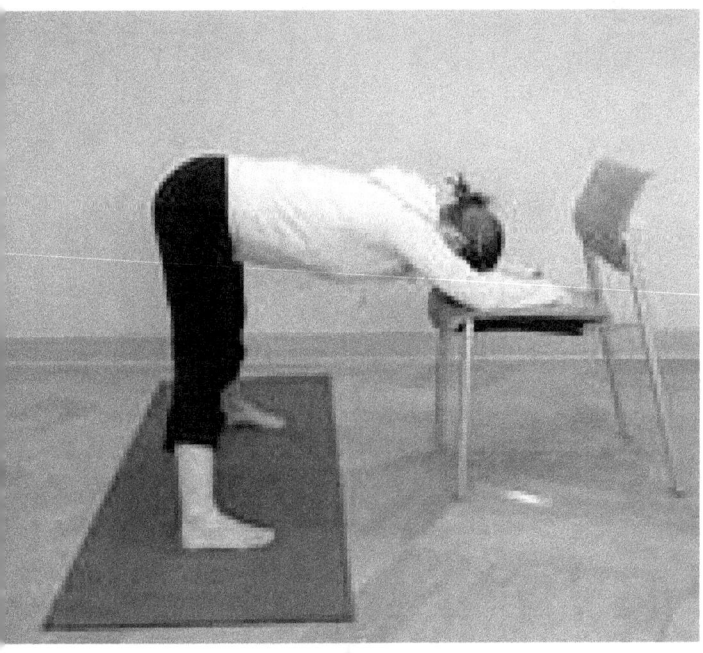

If you've been having trouble with your back muscles, then this pose will go a long way in remedying that. The forward bend pose is great for improving flexibility and strengthening the hips, lower back, and core muscles. It is beginner-friendly and can be done by just about anyone. The pose is a variation of the forward lean pose, but instead of being seated during the workout, you remain standing.

Here is how you go about doing the pose.
1. Start by standing in front of a chair facing it, with your back straight.
2. Take a deep breath, slowly lower your upper body as low as possible, and place your arms on the seat.
3. Once you cross your arms on the chair in front of you, lay your head on your hands and remain in that position.
4. Make sure you keep your legs straight: don't bend your knees.
5. Stay in that position for 20 seconds before returning to your original position. Repeat the same procedure for about 20 reps until you feel the tension released from your back.

#: Standing Leg Lifts

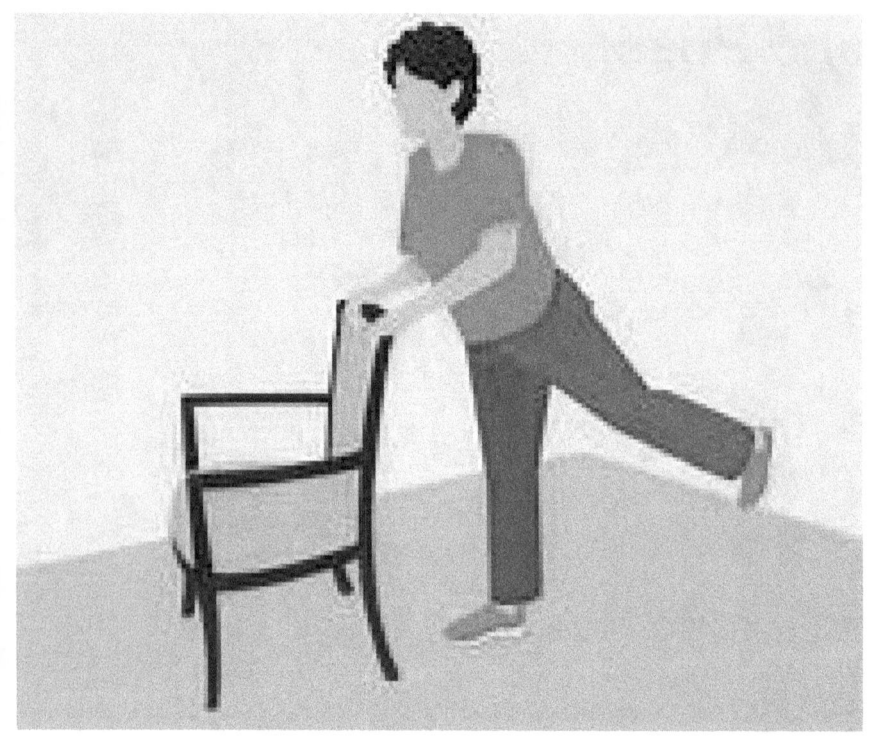

The standing leg lifts chair pose is a variation of the normal leg lifts, but thanks to the chair, the process becomes easier. This pose is great for opening up your body for a workout session, making this pose ideal as a pre-workout routine.

It is also great for improving flexibility and helps strengthen muscles in your body, such as the gluteus, hip, and calf muscles. It is quite easy and beginner-friendly so people of all levels can do it.

Here is how you go about doing the pose.
1. Start by standing in front of a chair with its back resting facing you.
2. Place your left arm atop the backrest, then take a deep breath.
3. Slowly as you exhale, lift your right leg and bring your right hand back to hold the leg at your feet.
4. Make sure to lift your right leg as much as possible and keep your left leg straight.
5. Remain in that position for about 20 seconds before repeating the same procedure with your other side.
6. Continue with the same procedure for about ten reps.

#: Standing Leg Stretch Chair Pose

The standing leg stretch pose is another great way to stretch and strengthen your glutes, hips, and lower back muscles. This chair yoga pose is beginner-friendly and helps improve flexibility in your lower body.

Here is how you go about doing the pose.

1. Begin by standing in front of the chair with your back straight.
2. Now carefully lift your left leg and place it on the seat while keeping it as straight as possible. Also, make sure your right leg is straight: do not bend your knee.
3. Bring your arms backward and cross them behind you, then lower your head down until your forehead touches your knees.
4. Remain in that position for about 20 seconds before repeating the same procedure with your other leg.
5. Continue with the same process for ten reps.

#: Triangle Pose

This is a beginner-friendly chair yoga pose that is great for improving flexibility and strengthening your core, leg, and arms muscles. It is also great for improving circulation and stretching your body in readiness for the workout session ahead.

Here is how you do the pose.

1. Begin by placing the chair in front of you with the backrest facing you.
2. Slowly breathe in and place your left hand on top of the backrest.
3. Spread your legs as wide as possible, then twist your upper body sideways towards your right as much as possible.
4. Remain in that position for 20 seconds before returning to your original position.
5. Repeat the same procedure with your other side and keep alternating for ten reps.

#: Standing Side Twists

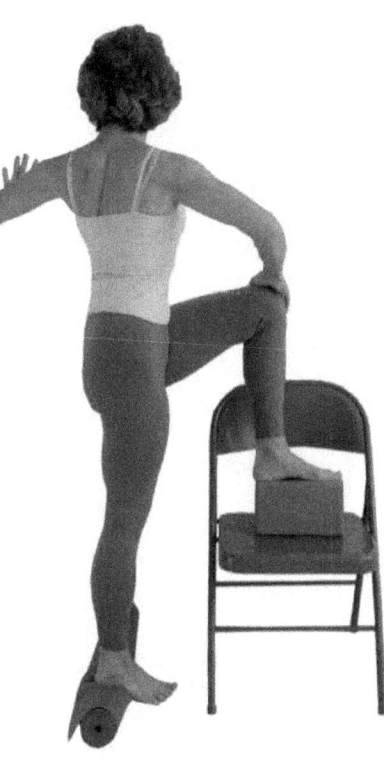

This variation of the seated side twists helps strengthen and stretch the lower back muscles, core muscles, gluteus, and arm muscles. The standing side twists are beginner-friendly and perfectly suited for seniors, especially because of the support chair. It is also great because, unlike the seated side twists, the standing side twists allow you to engage your lower abdomen.

Here is how you go about doing the exercise.

1. Begin by standing in front of a chair that is facing you. Ensure your back is straight and that you are facing forward before raising your left leg and placing it on your seat.
2. Place your left hand on your waist, then slowly twist towards your left as much as you can, then remain in that position for 10 seconds.
3. Now repeat the same procedure with your right side and pause for 10 seconds.
4. Change over to your right leg, then repeat the same procedure for about 10 reps.
5. Continue alternating from one leg to another for about 20 seconds.

#: Garland Hands-On Chair Pose

This exciting yet easy chair yoga pose is great for strengthening and improving flexibility in your lower abdomen muscles. Some of the muscles impacted by this exercise include the gluteus, core, hips, legs, and lower back muscles.

Thanks to the support provided by the chair, the chair yoga pose is quite easy and beginner-friendly. Unless you have a problem with your legs, you should easily do the pose.

Here is how you go about doing the garland chair pose.

1. Start by placing a seat right in front of you, then stand straight facing it.
2. Take a deep breath, then slowly lower your body down into a squat.
3. Breath out as you do so, then place both arms on the seat of the chair.
4. Remain in that position for about 20 seconds before returning to your original position.
5. You can also consider pulling one leg out as you squat to make the exercise more challenging

#: Upward Seated Straddle

The upward seated straddle is a variation of the seated straddle we discussed earlier. However, the difference between these two yoga poses is that the upwards one requires you to be on a seat, with your legs up in the air.

This chair yoga pose is great for strengthening and stretching your leg muscles, arm muscles, gluteus muscles, and lower back muscles. It is beginner-friendly and fun to engage in.

Here is how you do it.

1. Start by sitting in a nice and comfortable place.
2. Drive your legs as wide as possible, then slowly lift them in the air as much as you can.
3. Once your legs are wide and up in the air, bring your hands forward to try and hold them.
4. Remain in that position for about 20 seconds before returning to your original position.
5. Repeat the same procedure for about 10 reps.

Conclusion

As you can see, the chair yoga exercises in this book are not difficult and are perfectly suited for seniors.
The book contains detailed instructions on how to perform each of the poses, but the real work lies in doing them. All you need is a few minutes of your day to incorporate these poses into your daily routine, most preferably in the morning. With time, it will all become easier and a habit.
Good luck!

www.ingramcontent.com/pod-product-compliance
Lightning Source LLC
LaVergne TN
LVHW081525060526
838200LV00044B/2001